JOHN
BROWN

and the Fight Against Slavery

by James L. Collins

Gateway Civil Rights
The Millbrook Press
Brookfield, Connecticut

Interior Design: Tilman Reitzle

Photographs courtesy of: Corcoran Gallery of Art: cover;
Schomburg Center for Research in Black Culture: cover inset, 6,
7, 8, 22-23, 29; Steele Collection: 1, 9, 12; Baltimore & Ohio
Railroad Museum: 2-3; John Brown Farm Historic Site: 4, 30;
Library of Congress: 11, 13, 25 (top); Yale University Art
Gallery: 15; Kansas Historical Society: 16; National Park Service:
18-19; Gene Fellner: 21; National Archives: 25 (bottom);
Metropolitan Museum of Art: 27; Historical Society of
Pennsylvania: 28.

Cataloging-in-Publication Data

Collins, James L.
John Brown and the fight against slavery.

32 pp.; ill.: (Gateway Civil Rights)
Bibliography: p.
Includes index.

Summary: John Brown was one of the most daring men in the
history of civil rights. He hated slavery. His attempts to free
the slaves cost a number of lives and helped, indirectly, to
bring on the Civil War.
1. Brown, John, 1800-1859. 2. U.S. History – Civil War.
3. Abolitionists. 4. Civil Rights.
1991 B (92) Brown
ISBN 1-56294-043-0

At Harpers Ferry, John Brown made his final stand against slavery.

Men, are you awake?" John Brown asked as he paced back and forth in the darkness of the fire-engine house.

The day before, John Brown and his band of 21 men had raided the U.S. military post in the town of Harpers Ferry, Virginia. He hoped to capture weapons and use them to free the slaves in the area. He believed that the slaves would then join him in fighting for their freedom.

There had been shooting and killing on both sides, and several men had died in the fighting. John Brown and his men had taken 11 hostages during the early morning of October 17, 1859. But it was nearly a full day later now, and things were looking bad. Several of the raiders were dead, and others were wounded. Two of the wounded lay inside the engine house. One of them was Oliver Brown, one of John Brown's sons.

Oliver Brown was in a lot of pain because of his wounds. Finally, he could stand it no longer. He begged his father to shoot him, to put him out of his misery. But John Brown expected a lot from his boys. "If you must die," he told his son, "die like a man."

The prisoners looked at John Brown in surprise. "Gentlemen," he said to them, "if you knew of my past history you would not blame me for being here. I went to Kansas a peaceable man, and the proslavery people hunted me down like a wolf. I lost one of my sons there."

This statue of John Brown stands at
his family estate in North Elba, New York.

John Brown fought on while his men lay dying at his feet.

After a while, he called out Oliver's name, but there was no answer. Looking down, he saw that he had lost yet another son. "I guess he's dead" was all John Brown said.

When morning light came, John Brown and his remaining raiders took up positions at the gun ports of the engine house, sure they would have to fight their way out. They knew they were trapped.

Over the years, people have had different opinions about John Brown and the brutal methods he used to fight slavery. Whether he was right or wrong to act as he did, John Brown was one of the most daring men in the history of civil rights. This is his story.

The Early Years

John Brown was born in Torrington, Connecticut, on May 9, 1800. Like many children of his day, young John received most of his education from his parents. His parents used the Bible in teaching their son. They taught him to respect the word of the Bible and to believe in right and wrong. One of the greatest wrongs, they taught him, was slavery. The hatred of slavery would become a driving force in John Brown's life.

As John grew older, he learned the family's trade of tanning cowhides to make leather. At the age of 20, he married Dianthe Lusk, who gave him 7 children over their 12 years of marriage. After Dianthe died in 1832, John waited only one year before picking out another bride, 16-year-old Mary Anne Day. John Brown fathered 13 more children by her. As the children grew, John taught them all to hate slavery, just as his father had taught him.

John Brown was never much of a businessman. He established and then sold several tanneries. He bought and sold land. For a while he raised sheep. But he never made much money.

John Brown's tannery in New Richmond, Ohio.

Perhaps one of the reasons John was not a successful businessman was because he was so angry about slavery. He would sometimes visit blacks to find out how hard their lives were as slaves. When he left, he was always angrier than before.

In the 1830s, John Brown became more and more wild in his hatred of slavery. Once he said that he had spoken to God about the slavery problem and that God had appointed him to free the slaves.

When people heard that John Brown claimed he had talked to God, they began to think the man was crazy. When John's mother died, stories went around that she had gone insane. People wondered whether John Brown, too, was losing his reason.

But John Brown didn't care what these people thought. He had found his mission in life. He would dedicate himself to freeing the slaves.

The Abolitionist

John Brown was an abolitionist, a person who sought to end slavery. Abolitionists believed that no one should have the power to enslave another person. People who belonged to the abolitionist movement, which started in the early 1830s, believed that the Constitution of the United States guaranteed individual freedom to everyone, not just members of the white race. They demanded that slaves be set free.

John Brown claimed that God gave him the task of freeing the slaves.

After 1808, the slave trade was illegal, but owning slaves remained legal in the South. Many Americans thought that slavery would eventually die out, but they did not try to stop it. Then, in 1831, William Lloyd Garrison began publishing a newspaper called *The Liberator*. It was the nation's first abolitionist newspaper. Garrison's paper told Americans that slavery was a moral and religious issue. His words stirred up many Northerners, including John Brown.

Some abolitionists began a secret organization known as the Underground Railroad. This wasn't a real railroad, but a series of homes where runaway slaves could find shelter as they headed north to freedom. Harriet Tubman, a former slave, became famous for making many trips south to lead blacks along the Underground Railroad to freedom.

In 1844, John Brown moved to Ohio. There, he became active in the Ohio Underground Railroad. "No one would brave greater perils or incur more risks to lead a black man from slavery to freedom than he," one man said of John Brown. He went on to say that John would "come in at night with a gang of five or six blacks that he had piloted all the way from the river, hide them away in the stables maybe, or the garret." If anyone tried to take the blacks into custody, John Brown would "fight like a lion."

In 1849, John moved again, this time to North Elba, New York. A wealthy abolitionist, Gerrit Smith, had donated land there for a black community where free blacks could live in peace. John brought his family to live with the blacks to show that blacks and whites could live side by side.

Harriet Tubman

Harriet Tubman was born on a Maryland plantation in 1820. She grew up a slave, working in her master's fields, but she was a strong-willed woman who longed for freedom. Finally, in 1849, she escaped from the plantation and headed north to freedom.

But Tubman didn't forget about the slaves she had left behind. One year after her escape, she made a daring return to Maryland to help others escape. Tubman became a leader, or "conductor," on the Underground Railroad. Over the next 14 years, she risked capture and death as she led more than 300 people out of slavery.

In 1858, Harriet Tubman met John Brown at a gathering of abolitionists in Canada. He was impressed by her determination to keep fighting against slavery. He called her "General Tubman."

When the Civil War broke out, Harriet Tubman worked as a scout for the North, leading soldiers south to raid Confederate lands. Even after the North won the war, she didn't stop crusading. She joined the women's movement, which was then gaining in popularity. She worked with Sojourner Truth, Susan B. Anthony, and others to gain equal rights for women.

When Harriet Tubman died on March 10, 1913, she was one of the most respected women in the country.

135,000 SETS, 270,000 VOLUMES SOLD.

UNCLE TOM'S CABIN

FOR SALE HERE.

AN EDITION FOR THE MILLION, COMPLETE IN 1 Vol., PRICE 37 1-2 CENTS.
"   "   IN GERMAN, IN 1 Vol., PRICE 50 CENTS.
"   "   IN 2 Vols., CLOTH, 6 PLATES, PRICE $1.50.
SUPERB ILLUSTRATED EDITION, IN 1 Vol., WITH 153 ENGRAVINGS,
PRICES FROM $2.50 TO $5.00.

The Greatest Book of the Age.

Uncle Tom's Cabin
*was a best-selling book
in many countries.*

Compromise

The decade from 1850 to 1860 was a dangerous and frightening period. Nearly everything that happened then had an effect on the people of the nation and how they felt about the issue of slavery. Each event carried America one step closer to a civil war.

In 1850, Congress passed the Fugitive Slave Act. Under this new law, Northern officials were responsible for returning runaway slaves to their owners. Slaves had no rights and could not go to court to ask for protection. Southerners were pleased with this law, but many Northerners hated it. They refused to obey it, and after it was passed the Underground Railroad became even more active.

The Fugitive Slave Act disturbed many people. One of those people was the writer Harriet Beecher Stowe. She was so angry about the law, which would help slave owners, that in 1852 she wrote a book about slavery called *Uncle Tom's Cabin*. The novel painted such a dark picture of slavery that it aroused feelings in both the North and the South. The book was so popular that it was reprinted in many languages and even made into a successful stage play. *Uncle Tom's Cabin* had a strong impact on the slavery debate of the 1850s.

Harriet Beecher Stowe's brother, Henry Ward Beecher, was an equally famous abolitionist. He believed just as strongly that slavery was immoral and wrong. As an ordained minister, the Reverend Beecher passed the word on to his congregation, as well as to any other groups who would listen to him. By 1855, Beecher was calling for a militant approach to solving the question of slavery. In an emotional meeting in Plymouth Church in Brooklyn, the Reverend Beecher began raising money to purchase

Harriet Beecher Stowe, the author of Uncle Tom's Cabin.

Sharps rifles. Beecher stated that he believed this new, accurate rifle to be just as powerful and effective as the Bible, especially on the Kansas frontier. "There are times," said Beecher, "when self-defense is a religious duty."

After this, boxes of Sharps rifles shipped to the Kansas frontier were stamped "Bibles" so that they would not be intercepted. The rifles became known as Beecher's Bibles.

One person who would carry one of Beecher's Bibles was John Brown.

Kansas Battles

Kansas became a battleground for slavery. Abolitionists came to Kansas to claim it as a free state. Some proslavery people from Missouri who called themselves Border Ruffians also came. The two groups were bound to fight.

John Brown's sons—Owen, Salmon, Frederick, Jason, and John, Jr.—first ventured into Kansas in the summer of 1855. They settled at Osawatomie on the Pottawatomie Creek. The area was lovely, with thick stands of oak, cottonwood, sycamore, and black walnut trees lining the river. Besides, Osawatomie was only 30 miles south of Lawrence, which was the center of abolitionist activity. The brothers wrote to their father about the troubles in the area, and in October 1855 John Brown joined them in Kansas.

During the next seven months, tension built between the abolitionists and the Border Ruffians over the slavery issue. Then, in the spring of 1856, a lawman from Lawrence was killed. No one was sure who did the killing, but both sides were angry. In May 1856, more than 800 Border Ruffians rode into the free-state town of Lawrence and destroyed the town. They smashed the printing press of the local paper, tore down a hotel, and burned down homes of abolitionists.

John Brown would not stand for this. On the night of May 24, 1856, he took action. He gathered four of his sons and a handful of others and visited five proslavery neighbors. The women and children were spared, but the man of each household was ruthlessly killed by Brown and his men. This was John Brown's revenge against those who had raided Lawrence. The Pottawatomie Massacre, as it was called, was the beginning of the violence that people would refer to as Bleeding Kansas.

Border Ruffians fought to keep slavery legal in Kansas.

Bleeding Kansas

In Congress, Northerners and Southerners had long argued about slavery and states' rights. Northerners were against slavery and believed that new states should be free of it. Southerners thought that whites in the new states should be allowed to keep slaves if they chose. In 1854, Congress passed a law that was intended to please everyone. It was called the Kansas-Nebraska Act.

The act said that the territories of Kansas and Nebraska should be able to decide for themselves whether they wanted slavery. This angered Northerners, who felt that the new act would allow slavery to grow in the United States instead of dying out. People who supported slavery moved into Kansas to fight for the right to have slaves. Abolitionists moved in to fight against slavery. John Brown's Pottawatomie Massacre was one of the many bloody encounters that took place.

Finally, President Franklin Pierce sent federal troops to the territory to restore order. Many elections were held, and several constitutions were drafted, before Kansas finally became a state. In the end, it was decided that Kansas would be a free state. But by that time more than 50 people had been killed in the struggle known as Bleeding Kansas.

To some, John Brown was now a hero of the abolitionist movement. But to many others he was nothing more than a murderer. Either way, no one doubted that he was deadly serious about wiping slavery from the face of the earth.

A Wanted Man

After the Pottawatomie Massacre, John Brown was a wanted man in Kansas. In the fall of 1856, he returned to Ohio. But he was still committed to ridding the land of slavery. He set to work on a new plan. To anyone else it might have seemed insane, but to John it made all the sense in the world. He planned to free all of the slaves in the South in one massive uprising.

John Brown announced his plan at a convention of abolitionists in Ontario, Canada. He wanted to lead a band of raiders into the mountains of Virginia and Maryland, gather slaves from plantations and farms, arm them, and establish a "freedman's republic," in which freed slaves would control their own government. John Brown wrote a constitution for the new government, and the convention agreed to it. They elected him as the leader of the new nation.

John Brown convinced some leading abolitionists, called the Secret Six, to provide money for the plan and to find volunteers. Then, in the summer of 1859, he rented a farm in Maryland across the Potomac River from the town of Harpers Ferry. Harpers Ferry was the site of a federal armory, where the United States Army stored weapons and ammunition. John Brown was almost ready for action.

This aerial photo shows Harpers Ferry, West Virginia, as it is today.

Harpers Ferry

On the night of October 16, 1859, John Brown and 21 recruits sneaked up to the armory at Harpers Ferry. With him were three of his sons—Oliver, Owen, and Watson.

The tiny group of raiders seized the armory and arsenal. "I came here from Kansas," John Brown told a frightened watchman as they disarmed him, "and this is a slave state; I want to free all the negroes in this state; I have possession now of the United States armory, and if the citizens interfere with me I must only burn the town and have blood."

John Brown and his men took several more buildings before a shot was fired. At first there was confusion, but by morning the town was up in arms. Farmers and soldiers began firing at the small band of raiders. Soon John and his men retreated to the fire-engine house on the grounds of the armory. That night, John's son, Oliver, died a painful death.

During the 24 hours since the raid had begun, the nation had gone into a panic. Wild stories were told. People said that a slave revolt was in progress. This scared many people in both the North and the South, for everyone knew such revolts were often bloody.

On the morning of October 18, John looked out the window and saw a company of United States Marines, commanded by Colonel Robert E. Lee. With Lee was a young lieutenant named J. E. B. Stuart. Both Lee and Stuart would go on to become famous leaders in the Confederate army during the Civil War. Right now their purpose was to take back the engine house and capture John Brown and what remained of his raiders.

J. E. B. Stuart approached the engine house. Stuart gave John a note from Lee, ordering him to surrender. Lee's note said that he would be protected from harm and turned over to the authorities. But John handed the note back, stating that he would surrender only if he and his men were allowed to escape.

Suddenly, while John Brown and Stuart were talking, a trooper jumped away from the door, and marines and state militiamen stormed the fortress. The raiders fired back from inside. But the soldiers battered down the door and were soon inside. Two marines fell to the floor, but they were replaced by two more who didn't. In quick order, two of the raiders were bayoneted to death.

A young marine lieutenant struck John Brown with his dress sword before the old man could fire, and he doubled over. If the young marine had used his battle sword, which was much more sturdy, John would

have died then and there. Instead, he was beaten over the head with the sword until he was unconscious.

When it was all over, three local men and ten raiders, including Oliver and Watson Brown, were dead.

A modern artist's painting of John Brown and his dying sons.

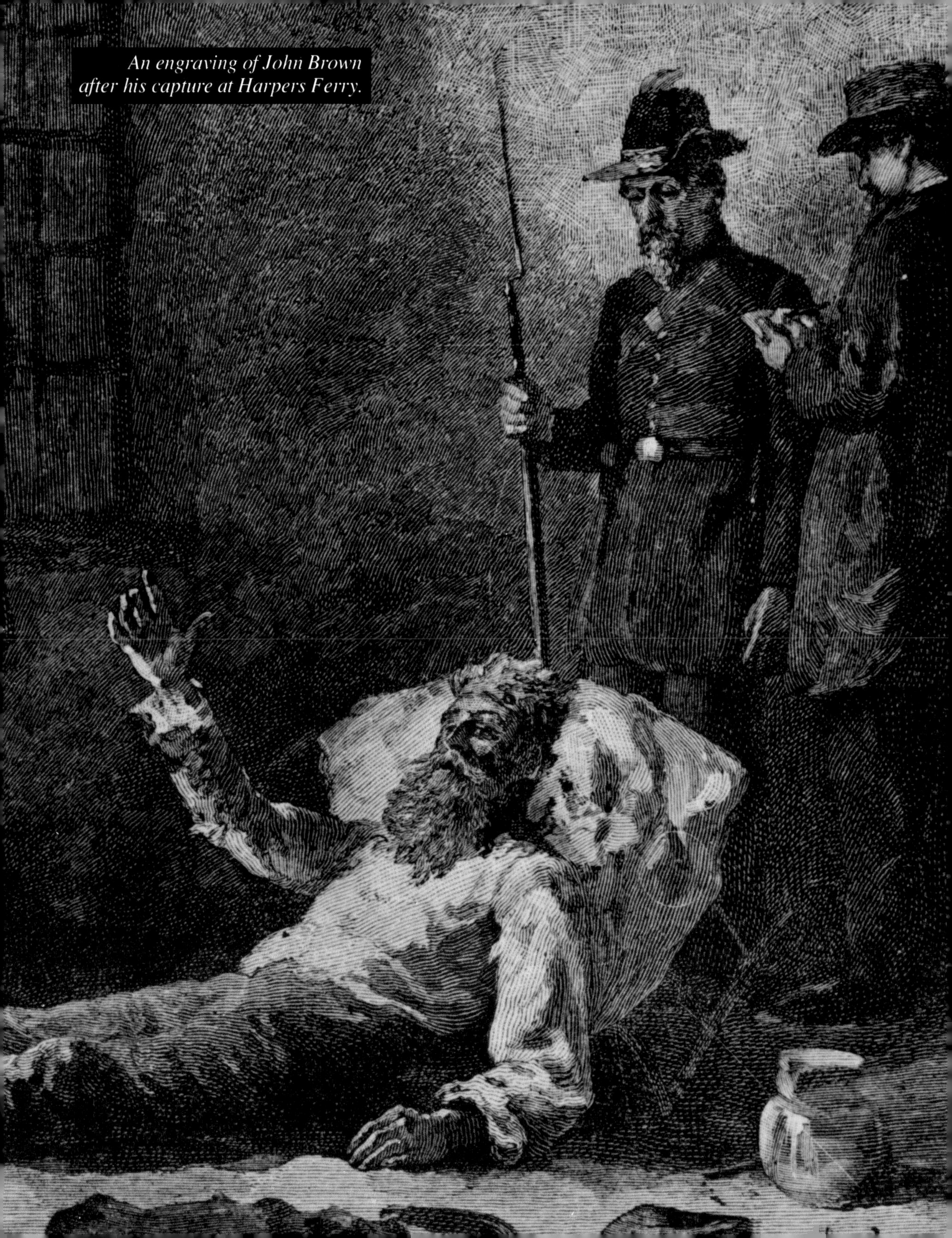

An engraving of John Brown after his capture at Harpers Ferry.

The truth of the matter was that John Brown's plan was unrealistic from the start. He had not told nearby slaves of his plot, and he had not developed an escape route. The plan to free the slaves of the South was heroic, but it was also hopeless.

When the fighting was over, the raiders were taken prisoner. John Brown had fought his last fight.

The Trial

On October 25, 1859, John Brown was put on trial. He was charged with the murder of four whites and one black, with helping slaves to rebel, and with plotting against the state of Virginia. The charge read: "The Harpers Ferry invasion has advanced the cause of Disunion more than any other event that has happened since the formation of the Government." How true those words were. This was the first time that the South had been attacked over the slavery issue. And the local population didn't like it one bit.

The trial itself was not long. Hatred for John Brown ran high, and the judge didn't want to give time for a mob to assemble. On November 2, just over a week after the trial had started, the jurors made their decision. It took only 45 minutes for them to find John Brown guilty of all charges. John seemed to be the only one who didn't show emotion when the verdict was read. It was almost as though he were looking forward to dying. He read a statement to the court, which ended:

The Dred Scott Case

Dred Scott

Before the Civil War, blacks almost never went to court to fight for their rights. One black man who did was Dred Scott. Dred Scott was a slave from Missouri who moved with his owner to a free territory. Scott claimed that since slavery was illegal in the territory, he should be a free man. The case went all the way to the United States Supreme Court.

On March 6, 1857, the Supreme Court ruled that Scott had no right to go to court because blacks were not citizens of the United States. They were property.

Southerners were pleased by the ruling. It reassured them that their slaves were property, and nothing more. But the ruling angered many Northerners who had not cared much about slavery before. The idea that the United States government considered human beings as property—no different from furniture or animals—made these people angry. They realized that the institution of slavery would not disappear on its own.

Thanks to the Dred Scott ruling, many Northerners decided that it was time to speak out against the evils of slavery. Along with John Brown's attacks, the Dred Scott case brought the nation closer to civil war.

Chief Justice Roger B. Taney ruled that Dred Scott had no right to sue for his freedom.

Now, if it is deemed necessary that I should forfeit my blood with the blood of millions in this slave country whose rights are disregarded by wicked, cruel, and unjust enactments, I say let it be done.

The judge sentenced the famed abolitionist to death. The hanging was set for December 2, 1859.

John Brown's lawyers spent the month of November rounding up statements from friends and relatives. They hoped to prove that he was insane. If they could do this, the death sentence might be changed. The many stories that the lawyers collected did seem to show that he was not very stable. But none of the statements were from reliable physicians, and the court did not reconsider the case.

On the day he was to be hanged, John wrote a message to his countrymen. It read: "I, John Brown, am now quite *certain* that the crimes of this *guilty land will* never be purged *away* but with Blood. I had *as I now think vainly* flattered myself that without *very much* bloodshed it might be done."

There was never any doubt about what John Brown believed in. There was never any doubt that he was willing to die for that belief. He fought slavery to the end.

Some people today think John Brown was a hero. Others think he was a madman. Whatever the case, his actions helped lead to the breakup of the nation. In November 1860, a year after the attack on Harpers Ferry, Abraham Lincoln was elected president. Southerners felt

This painting shows John Brown being led to his death.

Union troops marched into battle with John Brown's name on their lips.

that Lincoln would try to end slavery and so destroy their way of life. They decided they had to fight. On April 12, 1861, Southern soldiers fired on Fort Sumter, South Carolina, and the Civil War began. Four years of bloody battle lay ahead.

As the young Northern soldiers marched bravely into battle, they chanted a song to inspire them. It was called "John Brown's Body," and it was about the wild-eyed abolitionist who fought for his beliefs. The last line of the song is: "His soul is marching on."

Important Events in the Life of John Brown

1800	John Brown is born on May 9 in Torrington, Connecticut.
1820	John marries Dianthe Lusk, with whom he has seven children.
1832	Dianthe dies.
1833	John marries Mary Anne Day, with whom he has 13 children.
1849	John and his family move to North Elba, New York, to join a black community.
1855	John moves to Kansas to join his sons.
1856	John leads the Pottawatomie Massacre, in which five men are killed.
1858	John announces plans to found a "freedman's republic" in Virginia.
1859	John leads 21 men on a raid of Harpers Ferry, Virginia, and is captured.
	John Brown is hanged on December 2.

Find Out More About John Brown

Books: *Harriet Tubman* by Francene Sabin (Mahwah, N.J.: Troll, 1985).

John Brown of Harpers Ferry by John A. Scott and Robert A. Scott (New York: Facts on File, 1988).

The Story of John Brown's Raid on Harpers Ferry by Zachary Kent (Chicago: Childrens Press, 1988).

Places: The John Brown Museum is located in the Harpers Ferry National Historic Park, Harpers Ferry, West Virginia.

The John Brown Estate, located in North Elba, New York, contains John Brown's home and gravesite.

John Brown's house in North Elba, New York.

Index